GUINNESS WORLD RECORDS

GUINNESS WORLD RECORDS™

TOP 10

Awesome Ocean Records

Compiled by Laurie Calkhoven and Ryan Herndon

For Guinness World Records:
Laura Barrett, Craig Glenday, Stuart Claxton,
Kim Lacey, David Hawksett, Ben Way

SCHOLASTIC INC.
New York   Toronto   London   Auckland   Sydney
Mexico City   New Delhi   Hong Kong   Buenos Aires

Guinness World Records Limited has a very thorough accreditation system
for records verification. However, whilst every effort is made to ensure accuracy,
Guinness World Records Limited cannot be held responsible for any
errors contained in this work. Feedback from our readers on
any point of accuracy is always welcomed.

People like to explore all areas of their world, from the skies above to the oceans below.

This *Guinness World Records*™ book reveals the top ten record-holders in the watery world around us. Hold your breath and dive in!

ADVENTURE

Water covers about 71 percent of Earth's surface, which is more than two-thirds of our planet. Over 25,000 different kinds of fish call the ocean home!

How many oceans are there? One, four, or five are all the right answers!

The World Ocean (see chart below) holds all of the planet's seawater. Because the ocean is so huge, people think of it as many smaller seas with four main oceans — the *Pacific*, *Atlantic*, *Indian*, and *Arctic Oceans*. In 2000, a government group named the waters around Antarctica the *Southern Ocean*, which is now known as the fifth ocean.

Pacific Ocean	60,060,900 sq mi
Atlantic Ocean	29,638,000 sq mi
Indian Ocean	26,469,000 sq mi
Southern Ocean	7,848,000 sq mi
Arctic Ocean	5,427,000 sq mi

How do waves form? Fill a pan with water. Now huff, puff, and blow on the water — just like the wind does!

Strong winds make big waves. The highest recorded wave at sea was nearly as tall as 10 adult giraffes! This wave was 112 feet from trough to crest. **Trough** is the valley between two waves. **Crest** is the highest point of the wave.

Big waves make boats rock and roll. Sailors who can walk around during these storms have their "sea legs." Nobody was walking on deck when a huge wave rocked the U.S. Coast Guard's lifeboat *Intrepid* in 1971. This wave made the boat roll over in a full circle off the coast of Oregon.

Why is the ocean blue? (Mainly the ocean is blue because the sky is blue.) The ocean is like a mirror to the sky. On cloudy days, the water looks gray. Sometimes plants in the water give the ocean a blue-green color.

Why does ocean water taste salty? When water flows in rivers, it picks up salt from rocks and soil. This salted water flows into the ocean. Water evaporates into the sky and comes back as rain. The salt stays behind and the ocean gets saltier every day.

RECORD 1

Deepest Scuba Dive . . . By a Dog!

Scuba diving is a popular way to see ocean wildlife. But when Dwayne Folsom goes scuba diving off Grand Cayman Island, he takes his own animal with him — his dog Shadow!

Shadow is the record-holder for deepest scuba dive (13 feet) . . . by a dog! Shadow wears a special diving suit. Her jacket carries weights — 26 pounds — to help her 36-pound body stay underwater. She wears a plastic globe over her head, and her breathing tube connects to Dwayne's air tank.

Shadow likes to follow Dwayne everywhere. One day, Dwayne had gone scuba diving and Shadow jumped in after him! Dwayne built her special suit and taught Shadow how to scuba dive (right). Now they share many ocean adventures together!

EXPLORE

People first learned about the ocean by sailing and swimming. They wanted to know more, so they invented a *submarine*, a ship to go "under the sea."

When a submarine wants to *submerge*, or sink below the waves, its tanks fill with seawater. The added weight pushes the submarine *down*. When the submarine wants to *surface*, or go up, it pumps water out of its tanks. The air lifts it *up*.

Smallest Submarine

The world's smallest submarine is just big enough for one person.

The *Water Beatle* is only 9 feet 8 inches long and 3 feet 9 inches wide. It can dive to depths of 100 feet and stay underwater for four hours.

William G. Smith (below) uses this one-person sub to search for pieces of airplanes that crashed off the coast of England. The sub's first voyage was in 1993 to a depth of 80 feet.

The deeper a submarine dives, the darker the ocean gets. How do submarines see? They use sonar.

Sonar stands for **SO**und **N**avigation **A**nd **R**anging.

The ship sends out sound waves that travel through the water. The sound waves hit a target and bounce back to the ship. The ship measures the time it takes for the echo to bounce back. This is how they know where something is in the water.

Whales, bats, and dolphins use the same technique to find food for dinner! Echolocation is the name of their sonar.

Sperm whales (above) hunt using **echolocation**. The whale makes loud clicking sounds. The clicks travel through the water and bounce off objects — like giant squid (below) — telling the whale where its next meal is.

Deepest Dive by a Mammal

In 1991, a sperm whale (below) in the Caribbean Sea made the deepest recorded dive by a mammal. The whale dove to a depth of 6,500 feet! It took one hour and 13 minutes.

Maybe the sperm whale was hunting for its favorite meal — giant squid! These live in the deepest and darkest depths of the ocean.

Sharks don't use echolocation — but they can still catch and eat any prey they want.

Scientists built a shark-bite meter to test the strength of a shark's jaws. They hid the meter inside a fishy treat and tested the bite strength of different sharks.

The dusky shark's bite has a force of 132 pounds. At the tip of its teeth, that equals *22 tons of pressure.* It's the same as being

crushed by ten cars!

Bigger sharks have stronger bites. A great white shark (left) could eat a dusky shark for breakfast. No one has asked this shark to "bite down" on the meter — yet!

DISCOVER

People keep finding new and strange creatures living in the ocean. Sometimes, we even meet them eye to eye!

Giant squids (above) are mysterious creatures. Scientists are not entirely sure where they live, but they do know that they live deep down where it is very dark.

The Atlantic giant squid has the biggest eyes of any animal — living or extinct. A giant squid found in Canada in 1878 had eyes that were 15.75 inches in diameter. That's as big as an extra-large pizza!

All squids have eight arms, two long tentacles, and sharp beaks. They shoot out a cloud of dark ink. Giant squids can grow to be as long as a school bus and weigh close to 2,000 pounds.

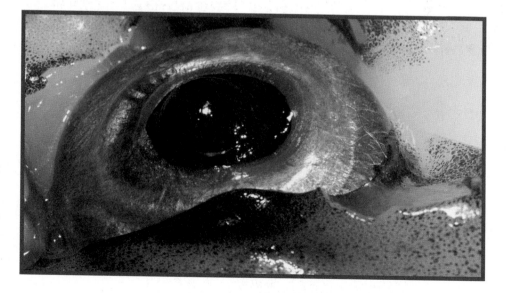

Longest Seaweed

Simple plants called **algae** live in the sea. **Kelp**, or **seaweed**, are types of algae. Clean water, sunshine, and cold temperatures help this plant grow quickly. The Pacific giant kelp (right) can grow 18 inches in one day and reach an outrageous length of 200 feet!

Thousands of animals swim around in kelp beds. Some live there. Snails, abalone, and sea urchins eat the plant. Others hunt there. Fish, sea stars, and sea otters hide in the kelp to catch their dinners.

Sponges aren't just things you use in the bathtub — there are such things as living sponges! These creatures live in the sea (left). In 1909, a wool sponge was found off the coast of the Bahamas. Wet, this giant sponge weighed 80 to 90 pounds. Dry, it weighed only 12 pounds. It measured six feet around! You can see this sponge at the National Museum of Natural History in Washington, D.C.

Crabs, lobsters, crayfish, and shrimps are **crustaceans**. Their outer skin is a hard crust, or **shell**, and it protects them from other animals.

The biggest crustacean is the Japanese spider crab (above). Its body is just 10 by 12 inches, but its 10 legs are 8 to 9 feet long. It can grow to be as big as a car!

Crustaceans are **invertebrate** animals. They don't have a backbone or spine. Other animals without backbones are worms and insects. Fish, reptiles, birds, and mammals (such as people, dogs, and whales) are **vertebrate** animals because they do have a backbone.

There are thousands of different kinds of fish. Scientists divide fish into two big groups: those with jaws and those without. Eels don't have jaws, but barracudas (above) do!

Fish with jaws are divided into two more groups. Fish with rubbery skeletons are **cartilaginous** fish. This means these fish have tough elastic tissue instead of bones. This is the same tissue that shapes your nose, ears, and throat. Sharks and rays are cartilaginous fish. **Bony** fish have skeletons made of hard bone.

Heaviest Bony Fish

The heaviest bony fish swimming in the ocean is the sunfish (below). Ocean sunfish can weigh as much as 4,400 pounds. They have one long fin on the top of their bodies and another on the bottom. From fin tip to fin tip, they can be 10 feet long.

Sunfish may be the laziest, too. Fish move their tails from side to side to swim. Whales, dolphins, and porpoises move their tails up and down. But sunfish simply flop onto their sides and float.

Largest Fish

The largest fish in the ocean is the whale shark (below). Its name is confusing. It is not a whale, but rather the biggest shark ever!

Whale sharks live in the warmer areas of the Atlantic, Pacific, and Indian Oceans. The biggest whale shark was caught in the Indian Ocean in 1949. It was 41 feet 6 inches long. That's longer than your school bus!

Whale sharks have 300 rows of tiny teeth but don't chew their food. They are **filter feeders**. These giant fish swim with their mouths wide open (above) and swallow water filled with tiny creatures named **plankton**. The whale shark's **gills** are like the bristles on a toothbrush. These bristles sort out, or **filter**, food from water. They swallow the plankton and push out the water through their gills.

Sailors believe dolphins bring them good luck. There are stories about dolphins that rescued people from shipwrecks and helped them swim to shore.

Dolphins are mammals, like us. They take in air through openings in their heads called *blowholes*. Whales breathe the same way. In fact, dolphins are small whales.

Dolphins live in seas all around the world. They are some of the fastest swimmers — they can swim up to 25 miles per hour!

Dolphins sometimes jump right out of the water (above). Spinner dolphins do flips and rolls in the air. Bottlenose dolphins have been trained to jump high. The Guinness World Record-holder managed to jump 26 feet from the surface of the water!

Humans have trained bottlenose dolphins to do more than tricks.

During the Vietnam War (1965–1973), the U.S. Navy trained five bottlenose dolphins to keep U.S. ships safe from enemy swimmers.

Dolphins also learned how to find underwater mines. When they found a mine, the dolphins released a balloon to mark the dangerous spot. In March 2003, dolphins patrolled the waters off Iraq, helping to keep U.S. boats safe (above).

The blue whale (above) is the biggest animal ever to live on Earth. It can weigh as much as 27 adult elephants (352,000 pounds)! Its heart is the size of a small car.

Blue whales are filter feeders. **Baleen** are the long bristles inside their mouths that filter the food from the water. Blue whales swim into groups of small sea creatures called **krill** with their mouths open wide. A blue whale can eat 40 million krill in one day.

It's no surprise the biggest animal makes the loudest sound! Blue whales (below) call to one another using loud moans. Their singing helps them swim closely together.

Sound is measured in decibels. A human whisper is 20 decibels. A blue whale's call is 188 decibels! That's louder than a jet engine.

Sound travels five times faster underwater than it does in the air. Using special equipment, scientists heard one blue whale's call up to 530 miles away.

Whales don't have vocal cords. So how do they make so much noise? Scientists think the noise comes from empty spaces inside a whale's head. Whales may push air from one space to another. If they do this fast, it might make an explosion of sound.

Humpback whales (above) "talk" more than other whales. They make squeaks, grunts, and groans. Male humpback whales even sing songs. Some of the songs are 20 minutes long. All the male humpbacks in the same area sing the same song together!